MEDITERRANEAN
VEGETARIAN
COOKBOOK

Plant-Based Recipes for a Healthy Heart
on a Mediterranean Diet

7-Day Meal Plan

Linda Gilmore

CONTENTS

Welcome

Are you looking for an approach to nutrition that goes beyond passing trends and that will improve your well-being and become an integral part of your daily routine? Consider the Mediterranean diet. Unlike fleeting fads focused solely on rapid weight loss, the Mediterranean diet offers a long-term approach to health based on the rich culinary traditions of the Mediterranean region. For generations, the people of this region have thrived on nutritional principles that promote longevity and healthy vitality.

Unlike restrictive diets, which often lead to short-term success, inevitably followed by failure, the Mediterranean Vegetarian Diet takes a holistic view of health. It does not advocate deprivation but instead celebrates the pleasures of plant-based foods with a focus on nourishing the body and taste. Whether you are a culinary explorer or a committed vegetarian, the Mediterranean Vegetarian Diet offers a variety of flavorful dishes that will delight your taste buds without compromising your values and health goals.

My journey is a testament to the transformative power of the Mediterranean Vegetarian Diet. I grew up in an environment that didn't prioritize the connection between plant-based eating and well-being. But when I discovered the wonders of this diet, it was a game-changer. Together with friends, we embarked on a culinary adventure, exploring new flavors and experiencing the health benefits of Mediterranean vegetarian cuisine. This diet not only changed my eating habits but also improved my overall health. With subtle adjustments to my diet, I lost weight and gained vitality and mental clarity.

Discover the secrets of Mediterranean vegetarian cuisine, embark on shared culinary adventures, and tap into a passion for a healthy and vibrant plant-based lifestyle. Join me on this journey where the Mediterranean vegetarian diet will become more than just a way of eating - it will become a transformative experience that nourishes body and soul, allowing you to enjoy life's moments to the fullest while staying true to your vegetarian values.

VEGETARIAN DELIGHTS IN THE MEDITERRANEAN SUN

Imagine this: you're strolling through a bustling market in Athens or meandering down a cobblestone street in Sicily, surrounded by the aroma of fresh herbs, ripe tomatoes, and pickled olives. It's like entering a gourmet paradise, where every corner offers a new discovery for your taste buds. And let me tell you, my vegetarian friends, the Mediterranean is a plant-based food lover's paradise.

I'll be honest, when I first started my journey to vegetarianism, my family and friends raised their eyebrows in bewilderment. "What about meat?" - they would ask, as if eating without meat was somehow incomplete. But let me tell you, once they tasted the incredible flavors of Mediterranean vegetarian cuisine, they were immediately hooked. And who can blame them for that?

You see, the beauty of vegetarianism in the Mediterranean lifestyle lies in its simplicity and abundance. It's not about deprivation or calorie counting; it's about rejoicing in the natural benefits of fresh, seasonal produce. From juicy tomatoes and crunchy cucumbers to creamy avocados and buttery chickpeas, the Mediterranean offers a treasure trove of ingredients just waiting to be turned into mouthwatering dishes.

One of my favorite aspects of Mediterranean vegetarianism is the emphasis on healthy, hearty meals that leave you feeling satiated and satisfied.

Take, for example, a classic Greek salad with juicy tomatoes, crunchy cucumbers, tart feta cheese, and juicy olives splashed with olive oil and a squeeze of lemon. It's like a party in your mouth, and trust me, you won't miss the meat one bit.

But perhaps the best part of being a Mediterranean lifestyle vegetarian is the sense of community and connection that comes from sharing meals with loved ones. Whether you're gathering around the table with your family for a leisurely Sunday lunch or hosting a holiday dinner with friends, food has the power to bring people together like nothing else.

I'll always remember the time I threw a Mediterranean-style feast at my daughter's birthday party. We made homemade hummus, plates of roasted vegetables, and stuffed grape leaves, and let me tell you, the kids couldn't get enough. They dipped, dunked, and devoured everything, and not once did they ask, "Where's the meat?"

So, my fellow culinary adventurers, if you are ready to embark on a culinary journey the likes of which have never been seen before, I encourage you to embrace vegetarianism as part of the Mediterranean lifestyle. Whether you're a seasoned vegetarian or just starting out, you'll find endless inspiration, flavor, and joy waiting for you in every bite.

VEGGIE BLISS

It all starts with limitations. Many of us have already realized that life is best lived when we limit ourselves from doing all the crazy, lazy, and stupid things of which we can think. But that doesn't mean you have to be miserable! No, please don't get me wrong. When I chose this path for myself, I had to lay the groundwork for my choice mentally. I really had to want it! Not just "try it."

The Mediterranean lifestyle has had an incredible impact on the health of people all over the world, no matter where they live. Consuming animal products (not from organic sources) has become the stigma of a healthy lifestyle in the 21st century. Replacing animal fats and proteins with plant-based fats and proteins isn't as tragic as you think, and I'm here to show you how.

Once you understand what macro and micro-nutrients YOUR body needs (everyone's metabolism is different), you can really dive into enjoying what you consume and see the results.

And the health benefits are tremendous! Especially for people with higher-than-normal blood fat levels, which, if left unchecked, leads to cardiovascular disease, Alzheimer's, Parkinson's, and type 2 diabetes over a lifetime. Benefits include:

SIGNIFICANT WEIGHT LOSS.

SIGNIFICANT REDUCTION IN INSULIN RESISTANCE.

IMPROVED BRAIN AND GUT HEALTH.

REDUCED RISK OF CARDIOVASCULAR DISEASE.

It took me six months to fully understand what my body needs, what it does, and why I should spread the word! But of course, sometimes the body can react negatively to restrictions. The most common negative effects are:

- B12, B6, iron, calcium, and zinc deficiencies
- Decreased energy
- Constant feelings of hunger

You may realize that by giving up animal products, you are automatically depriving yourself of some very important micro-nutrients that your body is used to. But during the first few months of practice, your body will readjust, and after a while, these problems should disappear. If you adjust your diet properly, these conditions usually disappear.

EXPLORING VEGETARIANISM

A vegetarian diet involves avoiding meat, poultry, and seafood, favoring plant-based foods. However, within vegetarianism, there are different dietary approaches that differ from each other in the inclusion or exclusion of certain animal products:

LACTO-OVO VEGETARIANISM is the most common form, which allows dairy products (lacto) and eggs (ovo) but excludes meat, poultry, and seafood.

LACTO-VEGETARIANISM is similar but excludes eggs while allowing dairy products.

OVO-VEGETARIANISM excludes meat, poultry, seafood, and dairy products but includes eggs.

The STRICTEST VEGANISM excludes all animal products, including meat, poultry, seafood, dairy, eggs, and often honey and gelatin, relying solely on plant sources.

Motivations for adopting a vegetarian lifestyle vary, including ethical considerations of animal welfare, environmental sustainability considerations, and perceived health benefits. Fruits, vegetables, grains, legumes, nuts, and seeds form the nutritional foundation of these diets, providing the body with essential fiber, vitamins, minerals, and antioxidants. Several studies indicate that a well-designed vegetarian diet can reduce the risk of hypertension, developing cardiovascular disease, type 2 diabetes, certain cancers, and obesity.

BREAKFAST

STRAWBERRY FRENCH TOAST

 **4 servings**

 10 minutes  12 minutes

Ingredients

4 thick bread slices (brioche/challah/ panettone)

3 whole eggs

1¼ cup (300 ml) whole milk

1 tsp. vanilla extract

¼ tsp. ground cinnamon

2 Tbsp. butter

sugar powder, Greek yogurt, for garnish

FOR THE FILLING:

2 Tbsp. strawberry marmalade

2 Tbsp. cream cheese

How to Cook

1. Cut a pocket in each slice of bread.

2. Fill each pocket with a quarter of the marmalade and cream cheese.

3. Whisk together eggs, milk, vanilla, and ground cinnamon in a bowl.

4. Coat each slice of bread with egg-milk mixture.

5. Melt the butter in a frying pan.

6. Toast each bread slice for 2-3 minutes per side until golden.

7. Serve warm, dusting with sugar powder and Greek yogurt.

Nutritional Info (per serving)

Calories: 370, Total Carbs: 26 g, Chol: 40 mg, Sodium: 1301 mg, Total Fat: 21 g, Protein: 20, Dietary Fiber: 8 g, Total Sugars: 5.4 g, Potassium: 704 mg

Here, I offer a recipe for a fairly traditional toast filling – marmalade and cream cheese. But I suggest you experiment with flavors and replace this filling with chocolate chunks and orange marmalade. And top the toast with orange slices poached with maple syrup in a skillet for a few minutes.

Toast with marmalade is great for Sunday family breakfast.

BRUSCHETTA WITH MUSHROOMS

 **2 servings**

 5 minutes   12 minutes

Ingredients

2 bread slices (baguette/
whole-grain/sourdough)

2 cups (250 g) mushrooms
(chanterelle/chestnut/
button), quartered

4 thyme sprigs

½ tsp. garlic powder

salt and pepper, to taste

1 Tbsp. olive oil

1 garlic clove

2 Tbsp. fresh parsley,
chopped

4 Tbsp. cream cheese
(optional)

How to Cook

1. Mix mushrooms, thyme leaves, garlic
   powder, salt, and pepper in a bowl.

2. Preheat your air fryer or frying pan to 390°F
   (200°C) and cook mushrooms for 10-12
   minutes until golden, stirring occasionally.

3. Meanwhile, toast the bread. Rub it with a
   garlic clove if desired.

4. Drizzle the toasted bread with olive oil
   or spread the cheese. Spoon over fried
   mushrooms.

5. Sprinkle with chopped parsley and serve.

Nutritional Info
(per serving)

Calories: 349, Total Carbs: 53 g, Chol: 40 mg,
Sodium: 1301 mg, Total Fat: 8 g, Protein: 20, Dietary
Fiber: 4 g, Total Sugars: 4 g, Potassium: 704 mg

Bruschetta is suitable as a quick and hearty breakfast or as one part of brunch. They are quick and easy to prepare from leftovers in the fridge. My favorite fillings are hummus with vegetables, tomato panzanella, pesto with nuts, or cheese and olives. I don't toast the bread too much, so it stays soft inside with a crispy crust.

The filling softens the bread, so the bruschetta should be eaten immediately. But the filling can be prepared in advance.

SPINACH FRITTATA

 **4 servings**

 10 minutes    20 minutes

Ingredients

5 whole eggs

1 cup (250 g) ricotta

3 spring onions

10 cups (300 g) mix of spinach, kale, and Swiss chard, chopped

¼ cup fresh parsley, chopped

¼ cup fresh basil, chopped

3 Tbsp. olive oil

salt and pepper, to taste

2 Tbsp. Parmesan slices, for garnish

How to Cook

1. Preheat your oven to 360°F (180°C).

2. Heat olive oil in the cast iron skillet over medium heat.

3. Add spinach and spring onion to the pan and cook for 3 - 4 minutes until tender, stirring occasionally. Remove the pan from the heat.

4. Add ricotta and herbs over the top.

5. Whisk eggs, pepper, and salt in a bowl. Pour into the pan over the greens and ricotta.

6. Bake for 20 minutes until the eggs are set.

7. Remove the pan from the oven and let it stand for 2-3 minutes.

8. Garnish with Parmesan slices and chopped greens.

9. Serve with crusty bread slices.

Nutritional Info (per serving)

Calories: 239, Total Carbs: 10.3 g, Total Fat: 17.4 g, Chol: 194 mg, Sodium 123 mg, Protein: 12.5 g, Dietary Fiber: 3.1 g, Total Sugars: 6.7 g

If you're a strict vegetarian and don't eat dairy products, you can replace them with vegan counterparts. Look for vegan cheeses and nut or coconut milk in your supermarket.

As for substituting toppings, there's no problem at all. Substitute spinach for asparagus, mushrooms with caramelized onions, sweet peppers, tomatoes, or green beans. Serve the frittata warm with a fresh, seasonal salad.

TURKISH EGGS

 2 servings

 10 minutes   7 minutes

Ingredients

2 medium eggs

1 red chili, finely sliced

1 garlic clove, crushed

1 cup (240 ml) Greek yogurt

½ lemon, juiced

2 tsp. sumac

salt and pepper, to taste

2 Tbsp. unsalted butter

2 Tbsp. fresh coriander/dill

How to Cook

1. Melt the unsalted butter in a small pan and add the sliced red chili. Cook for a few minutes.

2. Mix yogurt, crushed garlic, lemon juice, salt, and pepper in a bowl. Spread between two bowls.

3. Bring water to a boil in a small saucepan. Poach eggs in simmering water for 2 - 3 minutes until the whites are set.

4. Remove the eggs from the saucepan and put on the yogurt.

5. Drizzle the chili butter on top.

6. Sprinkle with sumac and coriander.

7. Serve with toasted bread slices.

Nutritional Info (per serving)

Calories: 340, Total Carbs: 13.3 g, Total Fat: 21 g, Chol: 402 mg, Sodium 223 mg, Protein: 26 g, Dietary Fiber: 3.7 g, Total Sugars: 9 g

I love eggs for breakfast in any form. Scrambled, boiled, poached eggs in water or olive oil, with cheese or vegetables - I love them all. This is my favorite product, and I am always looking for a new way to prepare eggs.

Turkish eggs, or cilbir, is a dish we inherited from the Ottoman Empire. It has only three main ingredients: eggs, yogurt, and chili oil. Poached eggs on garlic yogurt are drizzled with melted butter or olive oil infused with hot pepper. I pair the eggs with toasted bread, which can be dipped in the yolks and yogurt.

MOROCCAN CREPES

 **12 crepes**

 10 minutes (plus 30 minutes for rising)

 35 minutes

Ingredients

1 cup (240 ml) warm water

1 cup (240 ml) whole milk

1 cup (130 g) all-purpose flour

1 cup (180 g) semolina flour

2 whole eggs

½ tsp. sugar

a pinch of salt

½ tsp. active dry yeast

2 tsp. baking powder

½ cup (120 ml) butter

½ cup (170 g/120 ml) honey

vanilla extract

How to Cook

1. Mix the active dry yeast, sugar (of your choice), and water in a bowl. Let it stand for 5 minutes to dissolve the yeast.

2. In a blender, add yeast water, milk, flours, eggs, salt, and baking powder. Blend until smooth. Let it rest for 30 minutes.

3. Heat the skillet over low heat.

4. Measure out a quarter cup of batter and pour into the skillet. Cook for 3 minutes until the bubbles are set and the bottom is golden. Do not flip.

5. Blend the batter from time to time to keep it fluffy.

6. Microwave the mix of honey, butter, and vanilla extract until melted.

7. Serve crepes with honey butter sauce.

Nutritional Info (per serving)

Calories: 253, Total Carbs: 40.3 g, Total Fat: 10 g, Chol: 83 mg, Sodium 99 mg, Protein: 6.3 g, Dietary Fiber: 1.9 g, Total Sugars: 16.4 g

Baghrir, or crepes with a thousand holes was given to us by the ancient culture of Morocco and Algeria. This semolina crepe has a kind of exotic flavor. As befits an oriental sweet, they are extremely sweet. The sweetness is achieved by the sauce, which can be replaced with confiture or melted chocolate. Don't skip the sauce, please. It's worth it.

It is important to achieve the right texture of batter with bubbles, then the cooked crepes turn out airy.

APPETIZER & DIPS

BABA GHANOUSH

 4 servings

 **10 minutes**   **40 minutes**

Ingredients

1 medium eggplant (1 lb./ 450 g)

1 Tbsp. sesame oil

2 Tbsp. tahini

2 tsp. lemon juice

2 garlic cloves, peeled

1/8 tsp. salt

1/8 tsp. ground nutmeg

½ tsp. smoked paprika/ chili

2 Tbsp. fresh parsley, chopped

How to Cook

1. Preheat your oven to 425°F (220°C).

2. Wrap the garlic cloves in aluminum foil.

3. Poke the eggplant skin with the fork a few times and wrap it as well.

4. Roast the foil-wrapped garlic in the oven for 15 minutes and the eggplant for 40 minutes.

5. Let the eggplant cool, then peel and chop. Let it drain for 5 minutes.

6. Add the chopped eggplant, roasted garlic cloves, tahini, lemon juice, chopped parsley, salt, sesame oil, and nutmeg to the food processor and puree them.

7. Transfer eggplant puree to a serving bowl and garnish with paprika. Serve with pita, carrot sticks, or bell pepper wedges.

Nutritional Info (per serving)

Calories: 111, Total Carbs: 8.5 g, Total Fat: 7.6 g, Chol: 0 mg, Sodium 13 mg, Protein: 2.4 g, Dietary Fiber: 4.7 g, Total Sugars: 3.7 g

Baba ghanoush is a famous Lebanese dip where the main ingredient is roasted or fire-cooked eggplant. In its own way, it is a kind of classical chickpea hummus. You can also make hummus with avocado, pumpkin, peanuts, beets, or sweet potatoes. Find your favorite combination of spices and lemon juice.

If you can find smoked garlic, add it to the fresh, it's a nice addition as well (as is smoked paprika!).

GRILLED PORTOBELLOS

 **3 servings**

 5 minutes

 **7 minutes**

Ingredients

16 portobello mushrooms

3 slices bread

1 garlic clove

5 oz. (150 g) brie/
vegetarian brie, slices

4 Tbsp. pesto sauce

salt and pepper, to taste

olive oil, for drizzling

How to Cook

1. Preheat the grill to high.

2. Toss mushrooms, salt, pepper, and olive oil.

3. Arrange mushrooms on the baking tray and cook until soft, turning occasionally. Keep warm.

4. Toast the bread slices. Rub them with garlic, if desired.

5. Place the warm mushrooms on the bread slices, top with brie, and drizzle with pesto.

Nutritional Info
(per serving)

Calories: 392, Total Carbs: 29.4 g, Total Fat: 19.6 g, Chol: 73 mg, Sodium 686 mg, Protein: 28 g, Dietary Fiber: 4.7 g, Total Sugars: 2.1 g

There are recipes with stuffed mushrooms in every one of my books. I really love eating and cooking them. They are so calorie-dense that I have a hard time even categorizing them as appetizers. Stuffed mushrooms paired with a vegetable salad deserve to be a real dinner. They can be baked along with the stuffing or accompanied with soft brie cheese, as in this recipe. Cream cheese, feta cheese, tapenade, or any kind of risotto can be used as a filling.

ROASTED NUTS

 **1 cup**
4 servings

 **2 minutes**

 **5 minutes**

Ingredients

1 cup (130 g) raw almonds/
pecan/walnuts/cashews

FOR SWEET ALMONDS
(OPTIONAL):

sugar

cinnamon

pumpkin pie spice

FOR SAVORY ALMONDS
(OPTIONAL):
herbs

nutmeg

oriental spices/curry

onion/garlic powder

chili powder

olive oil/melted butter/
coconut oil

How to Cook

1. Preheat your oven or air fryer to 350°F (180°C).

2. Meanwhile, mix almonds with sweet or savory seasoning in a bowl.

3. Arrange them in a single layer in an air fryer basket or on the baking sheet. Roast for 5 minutes in an air fryer or 5-6 minutes in an oven. You can fry nuts for a few minutes in the skillet as well.

4. Don't forget to shake the basket 2 times during cooking.

5. Cool completely before serving.

Nutritional Info
(per serving)

Calories: 149, Total Carbs: 8.9 g, Chol: 0 mg,
Sodium: 0 mg, Total Fat: 12 g, Protein: 5 g,
Dietary Fiber: 3 g, Total Sugars: 4 g, Potassium: 174 mg

We always have a jar of crunchy nuts at home. Our family eats them both as a snack and as an addition to salads, breakfast granola, desserts, and baked goods. Also, my kids take them to visit friends and put them in cute little jars as gifts.

I mix the nuts with various coatings before roasting. After 5 minutes, the flavorful, crunchy nuts are ready. Roasted nuts have a brighter flavor than raw.

Cool the nuts completely before putting them away for storage.

Nuts contain healthy fats, vegetable protein and micro-nutrients, which makes this treat a great supplement for vegans, as well as adherents of paleo and keto diet.

DEVILED EGGS

 2 servings

 7 minutes   9 minutes

Ingredients

4 whole hard-boiled eggs, halved
2 Tbsp. mayo
2 Tbsp. Dijon mustard
½ tsp. paprika
1 Tbsp. parsley, chopped

FILLINGS (OPTIONAL):
feta cheese, crumbled

avocado, mashed

olives, chopped

fresh thyme, chopped

How to Cook

1. Cut boiled eggs in half and scoop out yolks.
2. Mix yolks, mayo, paprika, mustard, and the desired fillings in a bowl.
3. Stuff egg white shells with the filling.
4. Sprinkle with chopped greens or red pepper flakes.
5. Garnish with chopped parsley and serve.

Nutritional Info (per serving)

Calories: 306, Total Carbs: 1.4 g, Total Fat: 26.1 g, Cholesterol 379 mg, Sodium 488 mg, Protein: 15.5 g, Dietary Fiber: 0.3 g, Total Sugars: 1.4 g

Deviled eggs, or stuffed eggs, have a fascinating history. The ancient Romans enjoyed eggs seasoned with various spices, oil, and wine. The idea of stuffing egg whites with a mixture of yolks, spices, and other ingredients became popular in Europe as early as the 18th century.

During World War II, hard-boiled eggs gained even more popularity because of rationalization and the need to make do with limited ingredients. They were seen as a practical and economical dish that could be prepared from readily available ingredients.

Chefs and home cooks still experiment with boiled egg recipes today, adding ingredients such as cheese, avocado, and even sriracha to spice things up. Join in!

OLIVE TAPENADE

 **1 cup
8 servings**

 **7 minutes**   **0 minutes**

Ingredients

1 cup (135 g) Kalamata olives (green or black), pitted

3 garlic cloves

3 Tbsp. fresh parsley, chopped

2 Tbsp. capers

2 Tbsp. lemon juice

salt and pepper, to taste

rosemary, for garnish

How to Cook

1. Add all the ingredients to a blender except the olives. Blend until finely chopped.

2. Add olives to the blender and blend in short pulses.

3. Garnish with rosemary and serve with hummus, roasted bell peppers, or toasted bread.

Nutritional Info (per serving)

Calories: 96, Total Carbs: 17.4 g, Total Fat: 2.1 g, Cholesterol 0 mg, Sodium 888 mg, Protein: 4.5 g, Dietary Fiber: 3.3 g, Total Sugars: 1.3 g

The word "tapenade" comes from the Provençal word for capers, which are one of the key ingredients in the dish. The ancient Greeks and Romans made similar olive-based spreads, laying the foundation for what eventually became tapenade.

Legend attributes the creation of the tapenade to the Greek goddess Aphrodite. According to this myth, the tapenade was invented by her lover, the god Dionysus, as a sign of respect for her. He combined the best olives, capers, and herbs to create a true Mediterranean dish.

Today, tapenade is served not only as a spread but also as a sauce for pasta or as a topping for vegetables.

SALADS

SALAD WITH PEAS AND EGGS

 7 minutes    5 minutes

Ingredients

9 oz. (250 g) snow pea pods

12 quail eggs/4 small hen's eggs, hard-boiled

1 small bunch of lettuce, bite-size pieces

2 cups (50 g) fresh parsley

7 oz. (200 g) radish, diced

1 cucumber (100 g), diced

1 cup (50 g) arugula/baby kale, bite-size pieces

FOR VINAIGRETTE:

4 Tbsp. olive oil

1 Tbsp. lemon juice

1 Tbsp. orange juice

1 Tbsp. liquid honey

2 Tbsp. Dijon mustard

2 Tbsp. white wine vinegar

1 Tbsp. spring onion, chopped

2 garlic cloves, minced

salt and pepper, to taste

How to Cook

1. Combine all ingredients for the vinaigrette in a bowl

2. Add 4 cups of water to saucepan. Bring it to a boil. Add snow pea pods and cook for 1 minute. Take out and rinse in cold water for a few seconds to stop cooking.

3. Combine all the ingredients for the salad except the eggs. Pour over the vinaigrette and mix gently.

4. Top with sliced quartered eggs and serve on serving plates.

Nutritional Info (per serving)

Calories: 256, Total Carbs: 41.4 g, Total Fat: 6.1 g, Cholesterol 228 mg, Sodium 678 mg, Protein: 11.5 g, Dietary Fiber: 7.3 g, Total Sugars: 29.4 g

Before you start eating this salad, give yourself time to appreciate its colors and beauty. Here's a salad to toss together during the dog days of spring, when peas and radish are both at their best.

Customize it by adding any leafy greens you like. Bok choy, frisée, romaine, butterhead, iceberg, watercress, dandelion greens, or young cabbage leaves are all suitable.

LEVANTINE TABBOULEH

 2-3 servings

 10 minutes   0 minutes

Ingredients

1 cup (180 g) bulgur, cooked

3 cups (75 g) fresh parsley, finely chopped

1 cup (25 g) fresh mint, finely chopped

2 medium tomatoes, diced

1 small red onion (50 g), finely chopped

1 cucumber (100 g), diced

2-3 lemons, juiced

¼ cup (60 ml) extra virgin olive oil

Salt and pepper, to taste

How to Cook

1. Combine the cooled bulgur, chopped parsley, mint, tomatoes, onion, and cucumber in a large bowl.

2. Drizzle the salad with a dressing of olive oil, lemon juice, salt, and pepper.

3. Gently mix all ingredients so everything is evenly coated with the dressing.

4. Cover the salad and place in the refrigerator for at least 30 minutes to allow the flavors to mingle. Tabbouleh is best served chilled.

5. Stir the salad one more time before serving. Serve tabbouleh as a side dish, as part of a meze, or with pita bread.

Nutritional Info (per serving)

Calories: 160, Total Carbs: 24 g, Total Fat: 7 g, Cholesterol 0 mg, Sodium 56 mg, Protein: 5.5 g, Dietary Fiber: 7.7 g, Total Sugars: 8.4 g

Tabbouleh is a traditional Levantine salad that originated in the Eastern Mediterranean in countries such as Lebanon, Syria, and Palestine. In these regions, where summers are hot and dry, tabbouleh served as a refreshing and hydrating dish, rich in nutrients and flavor.

It is high in vitamins, minerals, and antioxidants found in fresh herbs and vegetables. Parsley contains vitamins C, K, and iron, while mint provides a refreshing flavor and aids in digestion. Olive oil provides healthy fats, and bulgur wheat adds fiber and complex carbohydrates, making tabbouleh a healthy and hearty dish.

BEETROOT ORANGE SALAD

 **2-3 servings**

 10 minutes  0 minutes

Ingredients

3 medium beetroots, boiled or roasted, peeled, and cubed

2 large oranges, peeled and segmented

¼ cup (40 g) pistachios/ pine nuts, toasted and roughly chopped

2 Tbsp. extra-virgin olive oil

1 Tbsp. balsamic vinegar

a bunch of arugula

1 cup (200 g) goat cheese/ blue cheese, cubed

Salt and pepper, to taste

How to Cook

1. Arrange the beet slices, orange slices, and arugula on a serving platter. Sprinkle the toasted pistachios or pine nuts on top.

2. Mix olive oil, balsamic vinegar, pepper, and salt until smooth.

3. Pour the savory dressing over the salad before serving. Add the cubes of goat cheese on top.

4. Serve immediately and enjoy!

Nutritional Info (per serving)

Calories: 274, Total Carbs: 16.4 g, Total Fat: 19.1 g, Cholesterol 26 mg, Sodium 188 mg, Protein: 11.5 g, Dietary Fiber: 3.7 g, Total Sugars: 12.2 g

The homeland of this salad is considered to be Greece and Spain, where beets and oranges are widely used in cooking.

An interesting aspect of this salad is the combination of sweet and salty flavors, which creates a harmonious balance. The earthy sweetness of the beets contrasts beautifully with the bright citrus notes of the oranges, and the addition of ingredients such as nuts, cheese, and tart dressing enhances the complexity of the flavor. Both beets and oranges are rich in vitamins, minerals, and antioxidants, making this salad not only delicious but also nutritious.

FATTOUSH SALAD

 3-4 servings

 10 minutes    10 minutes

Ingredients

2 whole-wheat pita breads

12 cherry tomatoes, halved

1 cucumber (100 g), diced

1 cup (100 g) radishes, diced

1 red onion (70 g), thinly sliced

1 cup (25 g) romaine lettuce / mixed salad greens, chopped

½ cup (15 g) fresh parsley, chopped

¼ cup fresh mint, chopped

¼ cup fresh cilantro, chopped

½ cup (70 g) Kalamata olives, pitted and sliced

1 lemon, juiced

¼ cup (60 ml) extra virgin olive oil

1 tsp. sumac

Salt and black pepper, to taste

2 Tbsp. pomegranate grains, for garnish

How to Cook

1. Preheat the oven to 350°F (175°C).

2. Divide the pita into two thin halves and cut into small pieces.

3. Toast bread pieces on a baking sheet in the oven for 10 - 13 minutes until crispy and golden. Let them cool.

4. In a large bowl, mix the tomatoes, radishes, red onion, cucumber, chopped lettuce, parsley, mint, cilantro, olives, and toasted pita pieces.

5. Whisk together lemon juice, sumac, olive oil, salt, and black pepper until smooth.

6. Add the savory dressing to the salad and stir.

7. Let the salad stand for about 5-7 minutes before serving.

8. Garnish with pomegranate grains. Serve the Fattoush salad as a refreshing appetizer or side dish.

Nutritional Info (per serving)

Calories: 287, Total Carbs: 46.9 g, Total Fat: 9.6 g, Cholesterol 0 mg, Sodium 419 mg, Protein: 9.5 g, Dietary Fiber: 10 g, Total Sugars: 11.4 g

Fattoush salad originated in the Eastern Mediterranean in traditional peasant cooking, where people used whatever fresh vegetables and herbs were on hand. I would call it a local adaptation of the famous Italian Panzanella salad. It, too, was born out of the need to use up leftover bread so nothing goes to waste. Adding crusty bread to the salad not only gives it texture but also enhances the flavor. Each nation adds those seasonal vegetables that are abundant. And flavors it with their traditional spices.

FRENCH POTATO SALAD

 **3 servings**

 10 minutes

 0 minutes

Ingredients

4 warm medium potatoes, boiled and sliced

2 cherry tomatoes, halved

12 radishes, sliced

1 cup (135 g) black olives

a small bunch of lettuce leaves, for garnish

10 cucumber pickles/ cornichons with dill (optional)

1 Tbsp. olive oil

1 Tbsp. vinegar from the pickle jar

How to Cook

1. Combine all the vegetables and olives in a large bowl. The potatoes are preferably still warm.

2. Mix the vinegar from the jar of cornichons with the olive oil in a small bowl.

3. Pour the dressing mixture over the vegetable salad and mix gently.

4. Serve on serving plates on a bed of lettuce leaves.

Nutritional Info (per serving)

Calories: 383, Total Carbs: 34.4 g, Total Fat: 26.8 g, Cholesterol 0 mg, Sodium 1768 mg, Protein: 5.5 g, Dietary Fiber: 10.3 g, Total Sugars: 10.4 g

Different dressings are pairs for warm salads, which perfectly emphasize the flavor of the main ingredients. Try Mustard Vinaigrette (Dijon mustard, white wine vinegar, olive oil, garlic or shallot, salt, and pepper), Creamy Mustard Dressing (Dijon mustard, crème fraîche, white wine vinegar, salt and pepper), or Lemon Vinaigrette (lemon juice, Dijon mustard, olive oil, crushed garlic, salt and pepper).

SOUPS & STEWS

CALMING GREEN SOUP

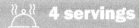 **4 servings**

 10 minutes   **30 minutes**

Ingredients

2 red onions (140 g), chopped

1 zucchini (150 g), chopped

1 large potato (300 g), peeled and chopped

9 oz. (250 g) frozen peas

14 oz. (400 g) baby spinach

2 garlic cloves, minced

2 tsp. cumin

20 g mint, chopped

5 cups (1¼ L) vegetable stock

1½ Tbsp. olive oil

½ cup (120 ml) Greek yogurt, to serve

pumpkin seeds, to serve

How to Cook

1. Heat the olive oil in a deep saucepan. Add the chopped onions. Cook for 4-5 minutes, stirring constantly.

2. Add the cumin, garlic, sliced zucchini, and potatoes. Cook for another 5-6 minutes, stirring occasionally.

3. Add the stock, salt, and pepper. Bring to the boil.

4. Leave to simmer for 10-12 minutes until the potatoes are soft.

5. Add the peas, mint, and spinach and cook for another 3 minutes.

6. Let the soup cool lightly and blend it in a blender to the desired consistency.

7. Serve with yogurt, pumpkin seeds, and mint leaves.

Nutritional Info (per serving)

Calories: 209, Total Carbs: 27.4 g, Total Fat: 9.5 g, Cholesterol 2 mg, Sodium 1046 mg, Protein: 11.5 g, Dietary Fiber: 8 g, Total Sugars: 10.1 g

A famous chef used to say that a good recipe starts with loving the person you are cooking for. The recipe for green soup has been passed down from generation to generation. The soup was said to be able to soothe the soul and bring peace to the mind. Each ingredient is a reflection of the vibrant Mediterranean landscape: juicy green spinach, tender peas, and fragrant mint, all harvested from your own garden.

Serve it with natural yogurt and a sprinkle of black pepper, garnishing each bowl with a few mint leaves. Your loved ones will appreciate the healing power of good food and a loving heart.

ITALIAN MINESTRONE

 **6-8 servings**

Ingredients

2 Tbsp. olive oil

1½ cups (200 g) onions, chopped

2 cups carrots (240 g), chopped

2 cups celery (200 g), chopped

2 cups (400 g) butternut squash, peeled and chopped

2 tsp. fresh thyme, chopped

3 garlic cloves, minced

1 can (26 oz./740 g) tomatoes, diced

9- 10 oz. (255 – 285 g) fresh baby spinach leaves

6-8 cups (1½ – 2 L) vegetable stock

1 bay leaf

Salt and black pepper to taste

1 can (15 oz./425 g) cannellini beans, drained and rinsed

2 cups (400 g) small-sized pasta, cooked

½ cup (120 ml) dry white wine

Garlic bruschetta/whole-grain Italian bread/ breadsticks

Parmesan cheese, shredded

 15 minutes

 40-50 minutes

How to Cook

1. Place a big saucepan over medium heat and add 2 tablespoons of olive oil.

2. Add chopped onions, celery, carrots, squash, minced garlic, and thyme. Cook for 6 - 8 minutes over medium heat until tender, stirring occasionally.

3. Add vegetable stock, 1 tablespoon of salt, bay leaf, and 1½ teaspoon of pepper to your pot. Simmer for 25 - 30 minutes, stirring occasionally.

4. Discard the bay leaf.

5. Add beans, cooked pasta, canned tomatoes, and more stock if desired.

6. Add spinach and white wine. Season with salt and pepper to taste.

7. Sprinkle with shredded Parmesan and drizzle with olive oil. Serve with garlic bruschetta.

Nutritional Info (per serving)

Calories: 296, Total Fat: 7.5 g, Saturated Fat: 1.9 g, Cholesterol: 21 mg, Sodium: 192 mg, Total Carbs: 49 g, Dietary Fiber: 10.6 g, Total Sugars: 8 g, Protein: 11 g, Vitamin D: 0 mcg, Calcium: 292 mg, Iron: 9 mg, Potassium: 1017 mg

The name "minestrone" comes from the Italian word meaning "soup". Minestrone was cooked in ancient Rome. The diet of the average Roman was predominantly vegetarian: onions, garlic, carrots, asparagus, mushrooms, and legumes. All of these were combined into a simple soup or broth. In the Middle Ages, more ingredients began to be added to the soup. In Liguria, pesto was added to minestrone, and in Tuscany, cannellini beans and cabbage.

The beauty of minestrone is its adaptability to the seasons. Spring minestrone can include fresh peas, asparagus, and young herbs, while winter minestrone can include root vegetables, kale, and beans. This seasonal approach ensures that the soup is always fresh and utilizes the best of what's available.

FRENCH RATATOUILLE

 **4 servings**

 15 minutes   **40 minutes**

Ingredients

1 Tbsp. balsamic vinegar

1 bell pepper (150 g), chopped

1 medium eggplant (400 g), chopped

3 ripe tomatoes, chopped

1 Tbsp. tomato paste

1 medium zucchini (350 g), chopped

3 garlic cloves, minced

¼ tsp. ground ginger

1 Tbsp. olive oil

3 Tbsp. scallions, finely chopped

½ tsp. dried oregano

¼ tsp. red pepper flakes

1+1/3 tsp. paprika

¼ cup (60 ml) red wine

salt and pepper, to taste

fresh parsley, for garnish

How to Cook

1. Heat olive oil in a large skillet or a Dutch oven over medium heat. Fry the scallions for 4-5 minutes until golden.

2. Add the sliced eggplant and garlic and sauté for 3-4 minutes. Reduce heat to medium-low.

3. Add the ground ginger, red pepper flakes, dried oregano, paprika, salt, and red wine and cook for 5-6 minutes, stirring from time to time.

4. Add the bell peppers, tomatoes, and zucchini and braise until the vegetables are tender.

5. If you like a more liquid stew, add more wine.

6. Add the tomato paste and vinegar. Season to taste. Cook for 5 to 7 minutes.

7. Let stand for 15 minutes before serving to allow the flavors to meld.

8. Sprinkle with chopped parsley.

9. Serve with poached or fried eggs, rice, or crusty bread.

Nutritional Info (per serving)

Calories: 109, Total Carbs: 14.6 g, Total Fat 4.1 g, Chol: 0 mg, Sodium 35 mg, Dietary Fiber: 4.3 g, Total Sugars: 8.2 g

Ratatouille originates from the Provence region of southeastern France. Traditionally, ratatouille was considered a peasant dish. It was prepared by farmers and laborers using summer vegetables, which they had in abundance. A famous animated movie brought new attention to this humble dish. The interpretation shown there is more refined and aesthetic, worthy of haute cuisine.

Traditional ratatouille is cooked over low heat so that the flavors have time to mingle. However, modern versions can be cooked more quickly while retaining the essence of the dish. It can be served hot or cold, as a main course, or as a side dish.

GREEK LENTIL SOUP

 3 servings

 10 minutes   40 minutes

Ingredients

1 bay leaf

1 cup (200 g) uncooked brown lentils

2 carrots (120 g), finely chopped

2 celery ribs (100 g), finely chopped

4 garlic cloves, minced

1 small lemon, juiced

3 Tbsp. olive oil

1 onion (70 g), chopped

2 sprigs fresh rosemary

1 tsp. sea salt

6 sprigs of fresh thyme

2 Tbsp. tomato paste

4 cups (1 L) vegetable stock

How to Cook

1. Heat the olive oil in a sauté pan over medium heat.

2. Add onion and cook for 5 - 6 minutes until golden. Add garlic and caramelize for 1 minute, stirring constantly.

3. Add tomato paste to the pan, stir, and cook for 2-3 minutes.

4. Add the rest of the ingredients (except the lemon juice), cover, and simmer for 20 - 30 minutes until the lentils are cooked through.

5. Take out the herbs and puree in a blender to desired consistency. You can leave it as is.

6. Add lemon juice and serve with garlic bread or cheese platter.

Nutritional Info (per serving)

Calories: 293, Total Carbs: 46.4 g, Protein: 11.8 g, Total Fat 9 g, Chol: 0 mg, Sodium 80 mg, Dietary Fiber: 18.3 g, Total Sugars: 7.8 g

Lentils have been cultivated in the Mediterranean as far back as 8000 BC. They provide vegetable protein, making this soup a hearty dish for vegetarians and vegans. Lentils and vegetables are high in dietary fiber, giving you a feeling of satiety. The soup is low in saturated fat and high in fiber, which will help lower cholesterol and support your heart.

Ingredients such as garlic, olive oil, and various herbs have anti-inflammatory properties.

The ease of preparation in one pot makes this dish convenient and affordable for home cooks.

TOMATO BEAN SOUP

 6-8 servings

 15 minutes

 35 minutes

Ingredients

2 Tbsp. olive oil

1 medium onion (70 g), chopped

2 garlic cloves, minced

1 small carrot (70 g), cubed

1 celery stalk, diced

1 small red bell pepper (100 g), diced

1 small zucchini (150 g), diced

1 medium potato (80 g), peeled and cubed

15 oz. (425 g) canned crushed tomatoes

3-4 cups (750 - 1000 ml) vegetable broth

1 (15-oz./425 g) can kidney beans, drained and rinsed

1 (15-oz./425 g) can black beans, drained and rinsed

1 (15-oz./425 g) can chickpeas, drained and rinsed

1 tsp. dried oregano

1 tsp. dried basil

½ tsp. dried thyme

½ tsp. smoked paprika

Salt and pepper to taste

1 cup (25 g) fresh spinach / kale, chopped

¼ cup fresh parsley, chopped

1 lemon, juiced

How to Cook

1. Heat oil in a large saucepan over medium heat.

2. Add the chopped onion and garlic. Cook for 5 minutes until translucent, stirring occasionally.

3. Add the cubed carrots, celery, and red bell pepper. Cook for 5 minutes more until vegetables are softened, stirring occasionally.

4. Add the cubed zucchini, potatoes, crushed tomatoes, and vegetable broth to the pot. Bring to a boil.

5. Simmer for 12 - 15 minutes until the potatoes are cooked.

6. Add the beans, chickpeas, and seasonings to the pot. Stir well to combine. Allow to simmer for 10 minutes.

7. Add the chopped spinach/kale and parsley. Stir to allow the greens to soften.

8. Add the lemon juice and stir. Adjust the amount of salt and pepper to your taste.

9. Garnish with fresh parsley if desired.

10. Serve hot with crusty bread.

Nutritional Info (per serving)

Calories: 310, Total Carbs: 50.4 g, Protein: 14.5 g, Total Fat: 8 g, Sodium: 799 mg, Dietary Fiber: 13.7 g, Total Sugars: 6.3 g

Despite the long description, this soup is very easy to prepare. You just add all the ingredients in the order that they are all equally cooked, and the flavors have time to mingle. It is best to let these soups stand for 30-60 minutes after cooking to redistribute the juices.

The flavor of vegetable dishes depends greatly on the quality of each vegetable. Choose seasonal organic vegetables from a local farm that smells of summer and sunshine.

PASTA & RISOTTO

VEGAN PAELLA

 15 minutes    50 minutes

Ingredients

2 Tbsp. olive oil

1 small onion (50 g), finely chopped

3 garlic cloves, minced

1 small red bell pepper (100 g), diced

1 small yellow bell pepper (100 g), diced

1 cup cherry tomatoes, halved

1 cup (175 g) zucchini, cubed

1 cup (125 g) button mushrooms, sliced

1 cup (160 g) edamame, shelled

1 cup (125 g) asparagus, trimmed and cut into 2-inch pieces

1½ cups (330 g) rice (Arborio/Bomba)

1 tsp. smoked paprika

1 tsp. turmeric powder

4 cups (1 L) vegetable broth

½ tsp. saffron threads (soaked in 2 Tbsp. of warm water)

Salt and pepper to taste

1 lemon, thinly sliced

Lemon wedges, for garnish

How to Cook

1. Heat olive oil in a paella pan or a large deep skillet over medium heat.

2. Add onion and garlic and fry for 4 - 5 minutes until softened and fragrant.

3. Add cubed bell peppers and cook for 3-4 minutes until softened.

4. Add cherry tomatoes, zucchini, mushrooms, edamame, and asparagus. Cook for 5 minutes, stirring occasionally.

5. Add the rice (Arborio/Bomba) and vegetables. Add the smoked paprika, turmeric powder and saffron threads along with the soaking water. Mix well.

6. Add vegetable broth and mix with the rice and vegetables. Bring the dish to a boil.

7. Reduce the heat to low and cook without covering with a lid. Do not stir the rice during cooking so that a crust forms on the bottom. Cook for about 20 minutes. The rice absorbs most of the liquid during this time.

8. Season with salt and pepper to taste. Arrange the lemon slices on top of the paella and cook for 5 minutes.

9. Let it stand for 5 minutes. Serve on serving plates garnished with lemon wedges.

Nutritional Info (per serving)

Calories: 316, Total Carbs: 51 g, Protein: 11 g, Total Fat: 8.4 g, Cholesterol: 0 mg, Sodium: 68 mg, Dietary Fiber: 4.9 g, Total Sugars: 4.6 g

Paella is a traditional Spanish dish. It gets its name from the special wide and shallow pan used for cooking it. The main ingredients of traditional paella are rice, saffron (it gives the rice its characteristic yellow color), and olive oil. Cooks usually use short-grain rice such as bomba or calasparra, which absorbs a lot of liquid and does not become mushy.

Although traditional paella recipes are based on meat or seafood, many vegetarian and vegan options use ingredients such as artichokes, bell peppers, green beans, and other vegetables.

2-3 servings

Ingredients

12 oz. (340 g) spaghetti

2 Tbsp. olive oil

2 Tbsp. butter

3 garlic cloves, minced

1 small onion (50 g), finely chopped

10 oz. (280 g) mushrooms (cremini, button), sliced

4 cups (120 g) fresh spinach

½ cup (60 g) Parmesan, grated

Salt and pepper, to taste

Red pepper flakes

Fresh parsley, chopped (for garnish)

SPAGHETTI WITH MUSHROOMS

 10 minutes   **35 minutes**

How to Cook

1. Pour water into a large saucepan. Add salt and bring to a boil. Add spaghetti to the saucepan and cook according to package directions until al dente.

2. Set aside 1 cup of water to cook the pasta, then drain the water from the spaghetti and set it aside.

3. In a frying pan, heat a mixture of olive oil and unsalted butter until the oil starts to bubble. Add garlic and onion to the pan. Fry for 2-3 minutes, stirring occasionally.

4. Add the sliced mushrooms to the skillet. Fry for 5-6 minutes until mushrooms are tender, stirring occasionally. Season the mushrooms with salt, pepper, and red pepper flakes.

5. Add the spinach to the skillet with the mushrooms. Cook for 2-3 minutes until the spinach has softened. Add the cooked spaghetti to the spinach and mushrooms.

6. You can gradually add a little water in which the pasta is cooked until you get the desired consistency. Sprinkle with grated Parmesan and mix well.

7. Serve the spaghetti garnished with fresh parsley and additional Parmesan cheese if desired.

Nutritional Info (per serving)

Calories: 494, Total Carbs: 73.3 g, Protein: 20.7 g, Total Fat: 14.5 g, Cholesterol: 17 mg, Sodium: 206 mg, Dietary Fiber: 6.2 g, Total Sugars: 5 g

Although pasta is often associated with Italy, its origins are very old and can be found in different parts of the world. The word "pasta" comes from the Italian word for dough made from durum wheat and water or eggs. There are over 600 different forms of pasta produced around the world. Each form has its own sauces and additives. Pasta can be made from a variety of ingredients, including wheat, rice, corn, and legumes.

Specially designed pasta dishes have been incorporated into the astronauts' meals to provide them with familiar and nutritious food.

RISOTTO WITH ASPARAGUS

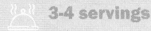 **3-4 servings**

 10 minutes   **40 minutes**

Ingredients

1 lb. (450 g) fresh asparagus, trim the woody ends and cut into 1-inch (1 cm) pieces.

1 cup (200 g) Arborio rice

1 small onion (50 g), finely chopped

2 garlic cloves, minced

1 cup (240 ml) dry white wine

4 cups (1 L) warm vegetable broth

½ cup (50 g) Parmesan, grated

2 Tbsp. (30 g) unsalted butter

Zest of 1 lemon

2 Tbsp. (30 ml) olive oil

salt and freshly ground black pepper, to taste

How to Cook

1. Pour water into a pot, salt, and bring to a boil. Add asparagus and cook for 2-3 minutes. Drain and set aside.

2. Meanwhile, heat the olive oil over low-medium heat in a sauté pan. Add the chopped onion and garlic. Cook for 5 minutes, stirring frequently.

3. Add arborio rice to the sauté pan and fry the grains in the oil for about 2 minutes, stirring often. Pour in the white wine and stir until it is absorbed into the rice.

4. Add the warm vegetable broth one ladleful at a time, stirring often and letting each addition soak in before adding the next. This process should take about 18-20 minutes.

5. Continue cooking until the rice has a creamy texture and is al dente. You may not need all the broth.

6. Add the blanched asparagus, butter, and shredded Parmesan cheese. The cheese and butter should melt.

7. Season with sea salt and black pepper. Add lemon zest for a fresh, bright flavor.

8. Serve the risotto immediately, sprinkled with Parmesan cheese, and drizzled with olive oil if desired.

Nutritional Info (per serving)

Calories: 407, Total Carbs: 45.1 g, Protein: 14.6 g, Total Fat: 16.6 g, Cholesterol: 25 mg, Sodium: 248 mg, Dietary Fiber: 5.9 g, Total Sugars: 5 g

I really love risotto for its creamy texture, mild flavor, and wonderful pairing with many spices and bright flavors. The creamy texture of risotto is not due to the addition of cream but to the unique properties of Arborio rice. Arborio rice contains starch, which is released with constant stirring and creates a nice creamy consistency. To make the right risotto, it is not only important to choose the right products, but also the cooking technique.

SPINACH RICOTTA CANNELLONI

 4-5 servings

 20 minutes    **75 minutes**

Ingredients

FOR THE FILLING:

18 oz. (500 g) fresh spinach, chopped

3 Tbsp. Parmesan, grated

9 oz. (250 g) ricotta cheese

1 garlic clove, minced

1 whole egg

1/8 tsp. nutmeg

sea salt and pepper, to taste

FOR THE SAUCE:

1 Tbsp. olive oil

1 onion (70 g), finely chopped

2 garlic cloves, minced

28 oz. (800 g) canned crushed tomatoes

1 tsp. sugar

sea salt and pepper, to taste

A handful of fresh basil, chopped

FOR ASSEMBLY:

9 oz. (250 g) cannelloni tubes

7 oz. (200 g) mozzarella cheese, shredded

Parmesan cheese, for topping

How to Cook

FOR THE STUFFING:

1. Boil or simmer the spinach for 2 minutes until softened. Allow it to cool.
2. Combine the spinach, ricotta cheese, egg, Parmesan cheese, crushed garlic, salt, pepper, and nutmeg in a bowl. Mix well until thoroughly combined.

PREPARE THE SAUCE:

3. Heat olive oil over low-medium heat in a sauté pan. Add onion and minced garlic and cook for 3 - 5 minutes until softened.
4. Add the chopped tomatoes, sugar, salt, pepper, and basil. Simmer the sauce for 15 - 20 minutes until slightly thickened, stirring occasionally.

ASSEMBLE THE CANNELLONI:

5. Preheat the oven to 180°C (350°F).
6. Meanwhile, spread a thin layer of tomato sauce on a baking dish.
7. Fill each cannelloni tube with the spinach and ricotta mixture. Place the cannelloni in a single layer in the baking dish.
8. Pour the cannelloni with the remaining tomato sauce so they are completely covered. Add shredded mozzarella and Parmesan cheese on top.
9. Cover the cannelloni with aluminum foil and bake for 25 - 30 minutes. Uncover the dish and bake for another 10-15 minutes or until the cheese is golden and bubbly.

Nutritional Info (per serving)

Calories: 467, Total Carbs: 37.5 g, Protein: 35.4 g, Total Fat: 21.7 g, Cholesterol: 143 mg, Sodium: 1208 mg, Dietary Fiber: 11.3 g, Total Sugars: 16.7 g

The cannelloni tubes can be boiled al dente, then filled, poured with sauce, sprinkled with cheese, and baked. You can choose any filling you like. Any vegetable pairs perfectly.

If the cannelloni tubes are difficult to fill, you can use lasagna sheets. Simply boil the lasagna sheets until cooked, place the filling along one edge, roll them up, and place them on a platter with the wrong side down.

MAINS & SIDES

4-6 servings

Ingredients

FOR THE FILLING:

2 eggplants, sliced

6 cherry tomatoes, sliced

2 Tbsp. olive oil

1 onion (70 g), chopped

2 garlic cloves, minced

1 carrot (100 g), chopped

1 red bell pepper (150 g), chopped

1 cup (210 g) dried lentils, rinsed and drained

14.5 oz. (400 g) canned diced tomatoes

2 Tbsp. tomato paste

1 tsp. ground cinnamon

1 tsp. ground cumin

½ tsp. ground allspice

1 tsp. dried rosemary

1 bay leaf

2 cups (500 ml) vegetable broth

Salt and pepper, to taste

FOR BÉCHAMEL SAUCE:

4 Tbsp. unsalted butter

¼ cup (40 g) all-purpose flour

2 cups (500 ml) warm milk

¼ tsp. nutmeg

½ cup (60 g) Parmesan, grated

1 whole egg, beaten

sea salt and pepper

FOR ASSEMBLY:

½ cup breadcrumbs

½ cup Parmesan, grated

MOUSSAKA

 15 minutes   **2 hours**

1. Preheat the oven to 400°F (200°C).

2. Drizzle the sliced eggplant with olive oil and arrange it on a baking sheet. Bake for 20-25 minutes until golden, flipping once halfway through. Remove from the oven and set aside.

3. Heat two tablespoons of oil in a deep-frying pan over medium heat. Add onion and fry for 3 minutes until tender. Add the minced garlic, carrots, and red bell pepper. Cook for another 5 minutes, stirring occasionally.

4. Add the lentils, canned tomatoes, tomato paste, cinnamon, cumin, allspice, rosemary, bay leaf and vegetable broth. Simmer for 25 - 30 minutes until the lentils are cooked and the mixture has thickened. Season with salt and pepper to taste. Remove the bay leaf and set the lentil mixture aside.

5. Add butter in a medium saucepan and heat it over medium heat until melted. Add the all-purpose flour and cook, stirring continuously, for 3 minutes until a smooth paste forms.

6. Gradually pour in the heated milk, continuing to stir until the sauce thickens. This should take 5-7 minutes.

7. Season with nutmeg, salt, and pepper. Remove the sauce mixture from heat and mix in the grated cheese. Allow the sauce to cool for a few minutes, then mix in the beaten egg.

8. Preheat the oven to 375°F (190°C). Grease a 9x13-inch (23x33 cm) baking dish with olive oil. Sprinkle the bottom with some breadcrumbs.

9. Arrange half of the roasted eggplant rounds in a single layer on the bottom of the baking dish.

10. Spread the lentil mixture evenly over the eggplant layer. Arrange the remaining eggplant and tomato slices on top.

11. Pour the béchamel sauce evenly over the top and sprinkle with Parmesan.

12. Bake for 30-40 minutes until the top is golden brown and bubbling.

Nutritional Info (per serving)

Calories: 594, Total Carbs: 56.7 g, Protein: 27.2 g, Total Fat: 30.6 g, Cholesterol: 151 mg, Sodium: 1396 mg, Dietary Fiber: 13.8 g, Total Sugars: 16.9 g

Moussaka is a traditional dish in the Balkans and the Middle East. Classic Greek moussaka consists of three basic layers: fried eggplant, a hearty sauce, and a creamy béchamel. Some variations include layers of potatoes or zucchini.

To simplify cooking, you can use a store-bought white sauce or make a quick version by whisking together milk, flour, and grated cheese until thickened.

Slice and salt the eggplants to draw out excess moisture. Then, instead of frying them, microwave them for a few minutes. This will shorten the cooking time and reduce oil absorption.

GREEK SPANAKOPITA

 **2-3 servings**

 15 minutes

 35 minutes

Ingredients

7 oz. (200 g) fresh spinach, chopped

1 cup (30 g) fresh parsley, chopped

6 oz. (175 g) sun-dried tomatoes with oil, chopped

4 oz. (100 g) feta cheese

2 whole eggs

5 oz. (125 g) phyllo pastry

How to Cook

1. Fill a large saucepan with water and bring it to a boil.

2. Add spinach and cook for 2 minutes. Remove from the sieve, leave to cool slightly, then squeeze out the excess water.

3. Mix the spinach, parsley, feta, and eggs in a bowl.

4. Roll out the phyllo pastry. Brush it with the oil from the sun-dried tomato jar.

5. Place it oil side down in a 9-inch (22 cm) pie dish so that part of the dough hangs over the side. Oil the next piece of the pastry and place it in the dish. Continue placing the oiled pieces of pastry into the dish until you have three layers.

6. Spread the filling over the dough.

7. Pull the dough from the edges to the center and pinch, covering the filling. Brush the top with oil.

8. Preheat the oven to 360°F (180°C). Cook for 30 minutes until golden brown.

9. Remove the pie from the baking dish, slice into wedges, and serve with seasonal salad.

Nutritional Info (per serving)

Calories: 264, Total Carbs: 26.8 g, Protein: 14.9 g, Total Fat: 11.5 g, Cholesterol: 208 mg, Sodium: 542 mg, Dietary Fiber: 2.5 g, Total Sugars: 3 g

Even the ancient Greeks and Romans made simple dishes with phyllo dough, which over time evolved into more complex creations such as spanakopita, or spinach, and feta cheese pie. The name spanakopita literally means "spinach pie" from the Greek.

Spanakopita is a popular vegetarian dish. Its main ingredients - spinach, feta cheese, onions or scallions, and eggs - make it a hearty and nutritious dish. Additional herbs such as dill, parsley or mint can be added to the filling, or nutmeg for extra flavor. Spinach provides vitamins A, C, and K, iron, magnesium, and dietary fiber. Feta cheese adds calcium and protein.

STUFFED BELL PEPPERS

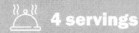 **4 servings**

 10 minutes   **40 minutes**

Ingredients

4 medium bell peppers (150 g each), wide and short

1 cup (160 g) couscous, cooked

1 small zucchini (120 g), chopped

1 small carrot (70 g), grated

1 white onion (60 g), finely chopped

1 cup (180 g) tomatoes, chopped

1 cup (160 g) canned chickpeas, drained and rinsed

1 garlic clove, minced

1/3 cup (50 g) pine nuts, toasted

2 Tbsp. fresh oregano, chopped

1 tsp. dried thyme

¼ tsp. ground nutmeg

½ tsp. allspice

¼ tsp. red pepper flakes

½ Tbsp. extra virgin olive oil

1 cup (120 g) Mozzarella cheese, grated

Salt, to taste

How to Cook

FOR THE FILLING:
1. Heat olive oil in a frying pan over low-medium heat. Add onion and fry for 3 minutes until tender.
2. Add garlic, zucchini, and carrots and cook for 5 minutes until softened, stirring occasionally.
3. Add the chopped tomatoes to the frying pan and fry for 2 to 3 minutes.
4. Add chickpeas, pine nuts, spices, salt, and pepper. Cook for another 2 minutes, stirring occasionally.
5. Remove from heat and add the cooked couscous, half of the grated cheese, and fresh oregano.

FOR THE PEPPERS:
6. Preheat the oven to 375°F (190°C).
7. Meanwhile, cut the tops off the wide bell peppers. Remove everything from the inside. Fill the peppers with the stuffing inside and cover with the cut tops.
8. Spread stuffed peppers on a baking pan. Bake for 15 minutes. Take the peppers out of the oven and remove the tops. Sprinkle the remaining grated cheese over the peppers. Return to the oven and cook for 7–10 minutes.
9. Serve warm sprinkled with fresh oregano or mint.

Nutritional Info (per serving)

Calories: 308, Total Carbs: 42.2 g, Protein: 11 g, Total Fat: 12.5 g, Cholesterol: 5 mg, Sodium: 258 mg, Dietary Fiber: 8.1 g, Total Sugars: 10 g

Try other vegetables suitable for stuffing, such as zucchini, eggplant, or even cabbage leaves. Simply hollow out or blanch your vegetable before stuffing.

Substitute couscous with any grain of your choice. Quinoa, bulgur, or even farro are great alternatives. For extra richness, add a handful of raisins or dried cranberries to the couscous mixture. This will add a sweet contrast to the savory ingredients.

You can substitute mozzarella with other cheeses such as feta, goat cheese, or grated Parmesan.

BROCCOLI CASSEROLE

 **4 servings**

 10 minutes 30 minutes

Ingredients

1 small red onion (50 g), sliced

2 garlic cloves, minced

1 bell pepper (150 g), chopped

1 cup (180 g) cherry tomatoes, halved

1 cup (90 g) broccoli florets

1 cup (175 g) zucchini, sliced

1 cup (30 g) fresh spinach

½ cup (60 g) feta cheese, crumbled

6 whole eggs

½ cup (120 ml) milk (dairy/plant-based)

1 tsp. dried oregano

1 tsp. dried basil

1 Tbsp. olive oil

salt and pepper, to taste

Fresh basil, for garnish

How to Cook

1. Preheat the oven to 375°F (190°C).

2. Meanwhile, grease a baking dish (9x9 inches /23x23 cm) with olive oil.

3. Arrange the chopped vegetables and spinach in the dish.

4. Sprinkle crumbled feta cheese over the vegetables.

5. In a large bowl, whisk eggs, milk, oregano, basil, salt, and black pepper until smooth.

6. Pour the egg-milk mixture over the vegetables and cheese in the baking dish, making sure everything is evenly coated.

7. Bake for 25-30 minutes, until the casserole is risen and golden brown.

8. Serve, garnished with basil leaves, paired with a crust of bread.

Nutritional Info (per serving)

Calories: 344, Total Carbs: 13.2 g, Protein: 25.1 g, Total Fat: 22.5 g, Cholesterol: 572 mg, Sodium: 399 mg, Dietary Fiber: 3.3 g, Total Sugars: 7.4 g

The word "casserole" comes from the French word for "sauté pan." Casseroles are prized for being cooked in one pot, making them ideal for family cooking and easier to clean up. They can be adapted to a variety of diets, including vegetarian, vegan, gluten-free, and low-carb diets.

Casseroles combine protein, vegetables, and carbohydrates, making them a balanced meal option. Ingredients can be modified using lean proteins, whole grains, and a variety of vegetables like artichokes, asparagus, or mushrooms.

GARLIC POTATO

 2-3 servings

 5 minutes

 30 minutes

Ingredients

1 lb. (450 g) baby potatoes, halved

2 Tbsp. olive oil

1 Tbsp. fresh lemon juice

1 Tbsp. lemon zest

3 garlic cloves, crushed

1 tsp. dried rosemary

1 tsp. dried marjoram

a pinch of sea salt, and pepper

1 Tbsp. fresh dill, chopped, for garnish

How to Cook

1. Preheat your air fryer to 400°F (205°C) or oven to 380°F (190°C).

2. Pat your potatoes dry and toss in herbs, lemon juice, zest, garlic, and olive oil. Arrange the ingredients on a baking sheet or in your air fryer basket for cooking.

3. Cook for 15 minutes in the air fryer or 25 - 30 minutes in the oven, shaking the basket halfway through, until light golden brown.

4. Garnish with freshly chopped dill.

5. Pair garlic potato with creamy mushrooms and fresh salad.

Nutritional Info (per serving)

Calories: 134, Total Carbs: 16 g, Chol: 0 mg, Sodium: 14 mg, Total Fat: 7.2 g, Protein: 3.3 g, Dietary Fiber: 3.2 g, Total Sugars: 0.2 g, Potassium: 518 mg

My kids, quite reasonably, believe that the best way to cook baby potatoes is to air fry them. To get potatoes that are crispy on the outside and tender on the inside, we borrowed this recipe from Greece. Marjoram and rosemary can be substituted for the Greek spices.

Before I discovered this appliance, I thought the easiest and most elegant way to cook potatoes was to fry them, but the air fryer makes them caramelized. I also use it to make caramelized baby carrots (with orange juice, cinnamon, brown sugar, and red pepper) or beets. Crumbled feta cheese and diced olives are complementary garnishes.

GREEN-STUFFED CAULIFLOWER

 **3 servings**

 10 minutes   **30 minutes**

Ingredients

1 small cauliflower (300 g), leaves removed

1 cup (30 g) fresh chervil, chopped

1 cup (30 g) fresh tarragon, chopped

2 garlic cloves, minced

1 whole egg

4 oz. (100 g) feta cheese, crumbled

2 oz. (50 g) breadcrumbs

Olive oil

Salt, to taste

How to Cook

1. Cut the stem of the cauliflower to the level of the florets.

2. Immerse the cauliflower in a pot of boiling salted water for 3 minutes. Turn it over and cook for another 3 minutes. Let it cool.

3. Combine the chopped herbs, garlic, egg, feta cheese, and breadcrumbs, then season with salt. Stir until you have a smooth paste.

4. Preheat the oven to 180°C (350°F).

5. Using a pastry bag, fill the spaces between the cauliflower florets with the green filling until it is filled.

6. Place the cauliflower in a baking dish. Sprinkle it with olive oil and the remaining breadcrumbs on top.

7. Bake for about 20 minutes until the top is golden brown and the cauliflower is tender.

8. Cut into wedges and serve.

Nutritional Info (per serving)

Calories: 170, Total Carbs: 13.3 g, Chol: 115 mg, Sodium: 413 mg, Total Fat: 8.7 g, Protein: 6 g, Dietary Fiber: 1.6 g, Total Sugars: 2.3 g, Potassium: 168 mg

Stuffed cauliflower is perfect for a weekend dinner or a dinner party with friends. It takes a bit of work to prepare, but the result is worth it. The protein filling with cheese and egg makes it a complete meal. Yogurt sauce, pomegranate grains, and chopped parsley are suitable as accompaniments.

BUTTER SAVOY WITH SAUCE

 **4 servings**

 15 minutes   **35 minutes**

Ingredients

FOR THE CABBAGE

½ cup (120 ml) unsalted butter, softened

2 Tbsp. sun-dried tomato paste

1 lemon, seeds and flesh discarded, finely chopped

½ tsp. red pepper flakes, plus extra to serve

1 tsp. cumin

1 small Savoy cabbage (800 g), cut into 6-8 wedges

Flaked almonds, to serve

FOR THE YOGURT SAUCE:

1 cup (240 ml) plain Greek yogurt

1 garlic clove, minced

2 Tbsp. fresh dill, chopped

2 Tbsp. fresh parsley, chopped

How to Cook

1. Combine the softened butter, sun-dried tomato paste, chopped lemons, red pepper flakes, and cumin.

2. Preheat the oven to 360°F (180°C).

3. Spread half of the butter mixture over the baking dish. Arrange the cabbage wedges on top. Brush the cabbage wedges with the remaining butter mixture so they are well coated.

4. Add ½ cup (120 ml) of water to the dish to create steam during baking to keep the cabbage from drying out.

5. Cover the dish with foil and bake for 35 minutes.

6. After 35 minutes, remove the foil. Put the cabbage back in the oven and bake for another 15 minutes.

7. Meanwhile, mix the Greek yogurt with the garlic, parsley, dill, and salt in a small bowl.

8. Transfer the caramelized cabbage to a serving platter and drizzle with the garlic yogurt sauce.

9. Sprinkle with almond flakes and red pepper flakes to give the dish some heat and crunch.

10. Serve immediately along with the cooked rice.

Nutritional Info (per serving)

Calories: 200, Total Carbs: 5.9 g, Chol: 39 mg, Sodium: 198 mg, Total Fat: 17.2 g, Protein: 3.3 Dietary Fiber: 3.2 g, Total Sugars: 0.2 g, Potassium: 518 mg

Roasting the cabbage in butter allows it to remain juicy and acquire a caramelized crispness. The butter transfers the flavor of the spices and lemons inside the cabbage. If you cover the dish with foil first, the cabbage will be steamed, making it tender. Removing the foil later ensures beautiful caramelization.

This recipe can be used for other types of cabbage, such as Brussels sprouts or cauliflower. Serve the roasted cabbage with a simple side dish of cooked rice to soak up the flavorful juices. Baked cabbage with sauce is perfect for vegetarians as a main course.

POLENTA WITH MUSHROOMS

 2-3 servings

 10 minutes   **60 minutes**

Ingredients

FOR THE POLENTA:

1 cup (170 g) polenta (coarse cornmeal)

4 cups (1 L) water / water + milk / vegetable broth

1 tsp. sea salt

2 Tbsp. olive oil

¼ cup (30 g) grated Parmesan

2 Tbsp. unsalted butter

FOR THE MUSHROOM TOPPING:

2 Tbsp. olive oil

1 white onion (70 g), sliced

3 garlic cloves, minced

2 cups (250 g) mixed mushrooms (cremini, shiitake, and oyster), sliced

½ cup (30 g) sun-dried tomatoes, chopped

½ cup (70 g) olives, pitted and halved

1 Tbsp. balsamic vinegar

1 tsp. dried oregano

1 tsp. dried thyme

¼ cup fresh parsley, chopped

sea salt and pepper, to taste

FOR GARNISH:

microgreens, grated Parmesan or crumbled feta cheese, olive oil, Sesame seeds, Lemon wedges

How to Cook

1. In a large saucepan, bring water and milk or vegetable broth to a boil. Add the salt.

2. Gradually add the polenta, reducing the heat to low. Keep stirring to avoid lumps.

3. Cook the polenta, stirring frequently, for 30-40 minutes, until creamy.

4. Stir in the olive oil, Parmesan cheese, butter, and seasonings to taste.

5. Heat a large pan over medium-high heat and add the olive oil.

6. Add the onions and cook for 3 - 4 minutes until soft. Then add garlic and cook for 1 minute until fragrant.

7. Add the sliced mushrooms and cook for 8-9 minutes until they release their juices and begin to brown.

8. Add the sun-dried tomatoes, olives, oregano, thyme, salt, and pepper. Cook for another 3 to 5 minutes.

9. Add the balsamic vinegar and fresh parsley and cook for another 2 minutes.

10. Place the mushroom mixture on a bed of polenta. Drizzle with olive oil.

11. Garnish with micro greens, grated Parmesan, or feta cheese.

12. Serve with lemon wedges on the garnish for a fresh flavor boost.

Nutritional Info (per serving)

Calories: 287, Total Carbs: 17.3 g, Chol: 20 mg, Sodium: 218 mg, Total Fat: 22.9 g, Protein: 5.3 g, Dietary Fiber: 2.2 g, Total Sugars: 2.6 g, Potassium: 298 mg

If you like creamy polenta, like me, you may want not just to boil it in milk but add a few spoonfuls of cream at the end of cooking. Creamy polenta pairs well with spiced roasted mushrooms.

Feel free to experiment with different types of mushrooms. Garnish it at the end with grated cheese and sesame seeds for a spicy flavor.

This dish pairs well with a seasonal green salad or roasted vegetables.

BREAD, PIES & DESSERTS

 **8 breads**

Ingredients

FOR THE DOUGH:

1¼ cup (300 ml) water

3 Tbsp. extra-virgin olive oil

1 tsp. honey

4 cups (500 g) all-purpose flour

1½ tsp. active dry yeast

½ tsp. salt

FOR THE FILLING:

4 tsp. extra-virgin olive oil

½ cup (100 g) black/green olives, pitted and sliced

½ cup (100 g) soft sheep cheese, crumbled

coarse salt

SHEEP CHEESE FOCACCIA

 10 minutes (plus 1 - 2 hours for rising)    **12 minutes**

How to Cook

1. Combine flour, water, yeast, salt, oil, and honey in a bowl. Knead the dough by hand or using the bread maker. Allow it to rise for 1 hour.

2. Divide the dough into 8 equal parts and form mini flatbreads.

3. Place them on a baking sheet lined with oiled parchment paper.

4. Make indentations in the dough with your fingers for the butter and filling. Spread the olives and sheep's cheese evenly over the tortillas.

5. Sprinkle the breads with olive oil and coarse salt.

6. Cover with a towel and leave for 45 minutes to rest and rise.

7. Meanwhile, preheat the oven to 425°F (220°C).

8. Bake for 10 - 12 minutes until golden brown.

Nutritional Info (per serving)

Calories: 372, Total Fat: 15.4 g, Saturated Fat: 2.8 g, Cholesterol: 11 mg, Sodium: 248 mg, Total Carbs: 50 g, Dietary Fiber: 2.3 g, Total Sugars: 1 g, Protein: 9.2 g, Vitamin D: 0 mcg, Calcium: 83 mg, Iron: 4 mg, Potassium: 91 mg

Focaccia has been known since the time of the Etruscans and ancient Romans. The name comes from the Latin word "focus," meaning "hearth," indicating that traditionally this dish was baked on a hearth.

The ingredients of focaccia and pizza dough are similar but contain more oil, making its flavor richer and texture softer. The oil also contributes to the crispy crust that characterizes a good focaccia.

The traditional filling includes a simple mixture of olive oil, sea salt, and fresh herbs such as rosemary or thyme. Sometimes, whole or sliced olives are added. In southern Italy, fresh cherry tomatoes and oregano are also added. My favorite topping is caramelized red onions.

MINI BAGUETTES

 8 baguettes

 10 minutes (plus 2 hours for rising)

12 minutes

Ingredients

1+1/3 cup (320 ml) water

3½ cups (500 g, 14½ oz.) all-purpose flour

1 package active dry yeast

½ teaspoon salt

How to Cook

1. Knead the dough in a bread machine or by hand. The dough should be slightly sticky to provide a chewy texture. Allow the dough to ferment slowly. Let it rest for 45 minutes.

2. Place the dough on a floured surface and divide it into 8 equal parts. Form sphere-like pieces and let them rest for 5 minutes. Shape each piece into a long baguette.

3. Place them on a baking sheet lined with oiled parchment paper, cover them with a towel, and let them rest and rise for 40 minutes.

4. Preheat the oven to 425°F (220°C).

5. Slightly sprinkle each baguette with flour and make 3-5 diagonal incisions with a sharp knife.

6. Bake the baguettes for 10-12 minutes until golden brown.

7. Allow it to cool down on the grid. Baguettes are best eaten fresh.

8. Serve with fresh, softened butter or your favorite topping.

Nutritional Info (per serving)

Calories: 232, Total Fat: 0.7 g, Saturated Fat: 0.1 g, Cholesterol: 0 mg, Sodium: 149 mg, Protein: 7 g, Total Carbs: 48.3 g, Dietary Fiber: 2 g, Iron: 3 mg, Total Sugars: 0.2 g, Vitamin D: 0 mcg, Calcium: 10 mg, Potassium: 97 mg

The iconic French loaves are loved for their crispy crust and soft crumb. The word "baguette" means "stick" or "loaf" in French, reflecting its long, thin shape. In France, a traditional baguette must follow strict rules: it can only contain flour, water, yeast, and salt, with no additives or preservatives.

They are perfect for dipping in soups, sauces, or olive oil. Or for bruschetta with fresh vegetables. For a sweet treat, slice a baguette, toast to desired crispness, and spread generously with butter, jam, or chocolate spread. Leftover baguettes can be used to make croutons, bread pudding, or Panzanella salad.

PEAR CHEESE QUICHE

 **8 servings**

 15 minutes (plus 75 minutes for rising)

 30 minutes

Ingredients

FOR THE DOUGH:

1¼ cup (300 ml) water

3 Tbsp. olive oil

3½ cups (500 g, 15¾ oz.) whole grain flour

¼ tsp. sea salt

1 package active dry yeast

FOR THE FILLING:

5 pears, peeled, halved, and cored

5 Tbsp. lemon juice

1¾ cup (400 g) Gorgonzola cheese, crumbled

1+1/3 cups (300 g) full-fat cottage cheese

4 Tbsp. apple cider vinegar

2 whole eggs

ground nutmeg,

2 garlic cloves, minced

pepper and salt, to taste

How to Cook

1. Combine all the ingredients for the dough in a bowl. Knead it in a bread machine or by hand. Let it rest for 45 minutes.

2. Sprinkle the pear halves with lemon juice. Put them in a saucepan, cover with boiling water, cover, and cook for 5 minutes on low heat. Take the pears out and drain.

3. In another bowl, add Gorgonzola, cottage cheese, eggs, garlic, salt, pepper, and nutmeg and stir.

4. Roll the dough out evenly and place it (forming a board) in a baking dish lined with oiled parchment paper.

5. Cut the pear into thin slices and evenly place them onto the dough. Spread the cheese mixture over the pears.

6. Leave in a warm place for 30 minutes to rest and rise.

7. Preheat the oven to 400°F (200°C).

8. Bake for 25-30 minutes until golden brown.

9. Slice, serve, and enjoy!

Nutritional Info (per serving)

Calories: 559; Total Fat: 22.6 g, Saturated Fat: 11.2g, Cholesterol: 91 mg, Sodium: 873 mg, Protein: 26.9 g, Total Carbs: 70.4 g, Dietary Fiber: 13.5 g, Iron: 3 mg, Total Sugars: 13.4 g, Vitamin D: 4 mcg, Calcium: 300 mg, Potassium: 485 mg

Mediterranean quiche is loved by everyone because it's just your favorite filling in a basket made of a thin layer of dough so it doesn't fall apart. The dough can be whole grain or even phyllo in the Greek version.

The stuffing usually consists of traditional foods of the region, like olives, feta cheese, sun-dried tomatoes, spinach, artichokes, and fresh herbs like basil and oregano. They can be served hot or cold, making them a versatile dish suitable for a variety of occasions. They can be part of breakfast, brunch, lunch, or dinner and are often a popular choice for picnics and gatherings.

ITALIAN ALMOND PIE

 **6-8 servings**

 15 minutes (plus 75 minutes for rising)

 **30 minutes**

Ingredients

FOR THE DOUGH:

1 whole egg

1 cup (240 ml, 8 oz.) lukewarm whole milk

¼ cup (60 ml, 2 oz., ½ stick) melted butter

2 Tbsp. (50 g) white sugar

4 cups (500 g, 18 oz.) all-purpose flour

1 Tbsp. instant yeast

¼ tsp. sea salt

FOR THE FILLING:

7/8 cup (200 g, 7 oz.) butter, softened

3 cups (200 g) almond flakes

2 Tbsp. (50 g) white sugar

How to Cook

1. Combine warm milk, melted butter, egg, sugar, flour, yeast, and salt in a large bowl. Knead the dough by hand or in the bread maker until smooth and elastic. Cover and let it rest and rise in a warm place for 45 minutes, or until it doubles in size.

2. Preheat the oven to 400°F (200°C).

3. Knead the dough to let the air out. Roll it out evenly on a surface sprinkled with flour and place it in a baking dish lined with oiled parchment paper.

4. Spread very soft or melted butter over the dough. Press down on the dough with your fingertips to make some indentations. Sprinkle the dough evenly with the sugar and then the flaked almonds.

5. Leave the pie in a warm place for another 30 minutes to rest and rise slightly.

6. Bake the pie for 25-30 minutes or until golden brown.

7. Let the pie cool on a rack. Slice and serve.

Nutritional Info (per serving)

Calories: 547; Total Fat: 32.9 g, Saturated Fat: 14.8g, Cholesterol: 75 mg, Sodium: 226 mg, Protein: 11.5 g, Total Carbs: 54.1 g, Dietary Fiber: 4.1 g, Iron: 3 mg, Total Sugars: 12.4 g, Vitamin D: 26 mcg, Calcium: 99 mg, Potassium: 273 mg

Almonds have been cultivated in the Mediterranean for thousands of years since the time of ancient civilizations. It was used in various baked goods and desserts. In Mediterranean cultures, it symbolizes prosperity and good luck.

In Spain, there is a famous Tarta de Santiago; in Italy - cakes with frangipane (filling of almonds, butter, sugar, and eggs) or marzipan; in France - Galette des Rois with almond cream; in Greece - almond cookies Amigdalota with rose or orange blossom water, in Morocco - Kaab el Ghazal (crescent-shaped cakes with almond paste and orange blossom water).

Almonds are a healthy food that contributes to heart health.

 **6 servings**

Ingredients

FOR THE PANNA COTTA:

2 cups (480 ml) heavy cream

1 cup (240 ml) whole milk

1 Tbsp. gelatin

½ cup (120 g) white sugar

1 tsp. vanilla extract

FOR THE BERRY SAUCE:

1 cup (190 g) mixed berries (strawberries, raspberries)

¼ cup (60 g) white sugar

1 Tbsp. fresh lemon juice

¼ cup (60 ml) water

PANNA COTTA

 10 minutes   **15 minutes**

How to Cook

1. Combine gelatin and ¼ cup cold milk in a bowl. Allow it to soften for 5 minutes.

2. In a saucepan, combine heavy cream, remaining ¾ cup milk, and sugar. Heat the creamy mixture over medium heat in a saucepan, stirring occasionally. Continue heating until the mixture is hot and the sugar has completely dissolved, but do not let it reach boiling point.

3. Remove the saucepan from the stove. Add the softened gelatin. Stir until the gelatin is completely dissolved. Add vanilla extract and stir to combine. Pour the mixture into individual serving molds. Let them cool to room temperature, then cover and place in the refrigerator for at least 4 hours or until set.

4. Meanwhile, combine the berries, sugar, lemon juice, and water in a small saucepan. Cook the mixture over medium heat for 5-6 minutes or until the berries have softened and the sugar has completely dissolved. Using a blender, puree the berry sauce until smooth. Allow it to cool to room temperature.

5. To remove the jelly, dip the mold bottoms in hot water for a few seconds, then using a knife to help yourself, invert them onto plates.

6. Spoon the berry sauce over the panna cotta. Garnish with fresh seasonal berries and mint leaves if desired.

Nutritional Info (per serving)

Calories: 430; Total Fat: 30.9 g, Saturated Fat: 19.2 g, Cholesterol: 113 mg, Sodium: 52 mg, Total Carbs: 36.5g, Dietary Fiber: 0.7 g, Total Sugars: 33.4 g, Iron: 0 mg, Protein: 4.5g, Vitamin D: 58 mcg, Calcium: 102 mg, Potassium: 161 mg

A relatively modern dessert, panna cotta originated in the middle of the last century in the Italian region of Piedmont. It means "boiled cream" in translation. It is loved for its delicate texture, variation in flavors (almond, vanilla, coffee, fruit, chocolate), and ability to hold its shape.

It is an easy-to-make, but exquisite dessert served in restaurants around the world. It can be made lighter by replacing some of the cream with milk or using a low-fat alternative.

STRAWBERRY TIRAMISU

 4 servings

 15 minutes    **2 hours**

Ingredients

1 lb. (450 g) fresh strawberries, hulled and sliced

¼ cup (60 g) white sugar

¼ cup (60 ml) fresh orange juice

1 cup (240 ml) heavy cream, whipped

8 oz. (225 g) mascarpone, softened

½ cup (60 g) powdered sugar

1 tsp. vanilla extract

7 oz (200 g) ladyfingers/ savoiardi

Cocoa powder, for dusting (optional)

Fresh mint, for garnish (optional)

How to Cook

1. Combine the sliced strawberries, white sugar, and orange juice in a bowl. Leave for 30 minutes to let the juice run clear.

2. Whisk together the mascarpone, powdered sugar, and vanilla extract in a bowl until smooth. Gently add the whipped cream and stir to combine.

3. Spread a fine coating of the mascarpone mixture on the bottom of a glass or serving dish.

4. Dip each ladyfinger in the juice from the macerated strawberries and place on top of the mascarpone.

5. Place another layer of mascarpone mixture on top of the ladyfingers, followed by a layer of sliced strawberries.

6. Repeat the layers, ending with a layer of mascarpone and strawberries.

7. Cover and place in the refrigerator for 2 hours.

8. Sprinkle the top with cocoa powder, garnish with fresh mint and serve.

Nutritional Info (per serving)

Calories: 363; Total Fat: 15.6 g, Saturated Fat: 8.9 g, Cholesterol: 120 mg, Sodium: 89 mg, Protein: 8.5 g, Total Carbs: 48.5g, Dietary Fiber: 1.7 g, Iron: 2 mg, Total Sugars: 24.4 g, Vitamin D: 10 mcg, Calcium: 119 mg, Potassium: 229 mg

Traditional Italian tiramisu is made with coffee-soaked savoiardi cookies, mascarpone cheese, cocoa, and liqueur. This strawberry version replaces coffee with a fresh fruit flavor, making it perfect for spring and summer.

Italian mascarpone cheese is a key ingredient in tiramisu, giving it a rich, creamy texture. These light and airy savoiardi cookies perfectly absorb flavors without becoming too moist. It helps to create the layers in tiramisu.

ALMENDRADOS

 20 – 24 cookies

 10 minutes

 20 minutes

Ingredients

1½ cups (170 g) almond flour

½ cup (100 g) sugar

24 almonds (25 g)

1 whole egg, beaten

1 tsp. lemon extract

1 Tbsp. lemon zest

How to Cook

1. Preheat the oven to 350°F (180°C). Line a baking sheet with parchment paper.

2. Combine the beaten eggs, zest, flour, lemon extract and sugar. Knead the dough until smooth.

3. Measure the dough with a tablespoon, shape each cookie into an oval flat shape, and place them on a baking sheet. You should end up with 24 cookies.

4. Press almonds onto the top of each cookie.

5. Bake for 20 minutes and let it cool before serving.

Nutritional Info (per serving)

Calories: 38, Total Fat: 292 g, Cholesterol: 7 mg, Sodium: 4 mg, Total Carbs: 5.4 g, Dietary Fiber: 0.7 g, Total Sugars: 4.3 g, Protein: 1.6 g

This is a traditional Spanish cookie with a touch of Arabic cuisine that introduced almonds and gourmet sweets to the Iberian Peninsula.

Almendrados are served with aromatic coffee or a sweet wine such as Pedro Ximénez or Moscatel sherry, which enhances their delicate almond flavor.

LEMON RICOTTA CAKE

 **4 servings**

 10 minutes   **35 minutes**

Ingredients

3 egg whites, whisked

3 egg yolks, at room temperature

1/8 tsp. sea salt

¾ cup (180 g) white sugar

½ tsp. vanilla extract

1 cup (240 g) unsalted butter, melted

1 cup (130 g) all-purpose flour

1 cup (250 g) whole-milk ricotta cheese

2 lemons zest

1 tsp. baking powder

How to Cook

1. Combine all ingredients except egg whites. Mix well with the mixer. To keep the cake from turning out dense, don't over-knead the dough. Knead it until it is light and airy. Gently stir in the beaten egg whites.

2. Preheat the fryer to 320°F (160°C) or the oven to 360°F (180°C).

3. Oil the baking dish with olive oil and pour the batter into it.

4. Bake for 20 - 25 minutes in the air fryer or 30 - 35 minutes in the oven, checking for doneness with a toothpick.

5. Serve the cake with Greek yogurt or a scoop of vanilla ice cream.

Nutritional Info (per serving)
Calories: 583, Total Carbs: 50.2 g, Chol: 184 mg, Sodium: 324 mg, Total Fat: 39.3 g, Protein: 10.4 g, Dietary Fiber: 1.1 g, Total Sugars: 30.6 g, Potassium: 207 mg

You can get beautiful swirls on top of the cake by adding a simple lemon glaze before baking. Combine powdered sugar and lemon juice and then beat into the batter with a toothpick or skewer.

For extra moisture and lemon flavor, drizzle the cake with lemon syrup after baking. Prepare the syrup by boiling equal parts lemon juice and sugar until slightly thickened, then pour over the warm cake.

This cake is the perfect accompaniment for afternoon tea or as a light dessert after a Mediterranean-style meal.

7-DAY MEAL PLAN

MONDAY

Breakfast	Strawberry French Toast 12
Lunch	Greek Lentil Soup 54 + Mini Baguettes 90
Dinner	Moussaka 70 + Garlic Potato 78
Snacks	Roasted Nuts 28
Desserts	Lemon Ricotta Cake 102

TUESDAY

Breakfast	Spinach Frittata 16
Lunch	Levantine Tabbouleh 38, Calming Green Soup 48
Dinner	Spinach Ricotta Cannelloni 66, Salad with Peas and Eggs 36
Snacks	Deviled Eggs 30
Desserts	Panna Cotta 96

WEDNESDAY

Breakfast	Turkish Eggs 18
Lunch	Italian Minestrone 50 + Sheep Cheese Focaccia 88
Dinner	Vegan Paella 60
Snacks	Olive Tapenade 32 with Mini Baguettes 90
Desserts	Strawberry Tiramisu 98

THURSDAY

Breakfast	Bruschetta with Mushrooms 14
Lunch	Fattoush Salad 42, Tomato Bean Soup 56
Dinner	Broccoli Casserole 76, Garlic Potato 78
Snacks	Grilled Portobellos 26
Desserts	Almendrados 100

FRIDAY

Breakfast	Moroccan Crepes 20
Lunch	Salad with Peas and Eggs 36 + Risotto with Asparagus 64
Dinner	Green-Stuffed Cauliflower 80, Polenta with Mushrooms 84
Snacks	Baba Ghanoush 24 with Mini Baguettes 90
Desserts	Italian Almond Pie 94

SATURDAY

Breakfast	Spinach Frittata 16
Lunch	Beetroot Orange Salad 40, Greek Lentil Soup 54
Dinner	Spaghetti with Mushrooms 62
Snacks	Greek Spanakopita 72
Desserts	Panna Cotta 96

SUNDAY

Breakfast	Turkish Eggs 18
Lunch	French Potato Salad 44, Calming Green Soup 48
Dinner	Vegan Paella 60, Butter Savoy with Sauce 82
Snacks	Pear Cheese Quiche 92
Desserts	Lemon Ricotta Cake 102

This meal plan offers a variety of meals that balance protein, carbohydrates, and healthy fats with plenty of vegetables, fruits, and whole grains.

ABOUT ME

My name is Linda Gilmore. I am a food journalist and author. I am highly recognized for making culinary magic in my home kitchen. I am also a busy mom of two. This means I am always on the run and looking for any chance to save time and money. I am a foodie through and through at my core, and I have grown into an **advocate for the Mediterranean lifestyle**. With a passion for healthy living and first-hand knowledge of what it takes to stick to a successful lifestyle plan, I will guide you throughout this journey.

The Internet is full of all the information a person might need, but surfing for the right pieces takes a lot of time and effort. Looking for answers to my amateurish questions made me read through countless complex professional texts.

How much did I wish I'd had a book with simple step-by-step explanations? Perhaps, that is the main reason why I've written this one.

I hope this book will allow you to enjoy the Mediterranean lifestyle with someone special.

WHAT TO READ NEXT?

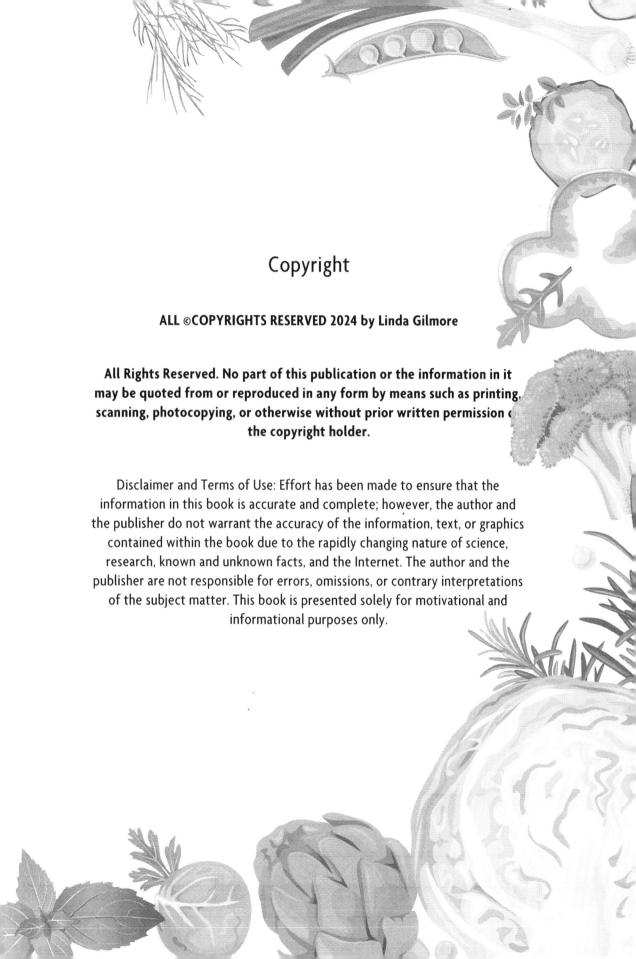

Copyright